Chocolate

Sweets & Treats!

A collection of delicious recipes for anyone who loves chocolate!

(im)PulsePaperbacks

Chocolate Pudding Melt/Serves 6

200g/7 oz dark chocolate
60g/2 1/2 oz plain flour
200g/7 oz butter, (cubed)
110g/4 oz golden caster sugar
4 large eggs and 4 large egg yolks
2 tbsps of brandy
2 tsps vanilla extract
Single or whipped cream for pouring, or vanilla icecream

Directions

1. Preheat the oven to 200°C/400°F/Gas mark 6. Break the chocolate into a bowl and add the brandy and butter. Heat over a pan of simmering water to melt slowly.

2. Once melted, remove from the heat and stir until smooth. Place the eggs, yolks, vanilla extract and sugar in a bowl and whisk using a hand-held electric whisk. Whisk the mixture until it has thickened to a mousse-like texture and doubled in volume.

3. Pour in the melted chocolate and fold into the mixture. Sift the flour into the bowl and then carefully fold all the ingredients together. It will take a few minutes to be mixed thoroughly. Spoon the mixture into 6 heat resistant pudding bowls and place them on a baking tray.

4. Bake in the centre of oven for 12-15 minutes, or until they have risen and are firm to the touch, (the centre of the puddings will be melting). Leave to stand for 2 minutes and then turn each pudding out onto individual plates. Serve straight away as a warm dessert with melting insides, or as a cold dessert with a fudge-like chocolate centre.

Continental Hot Chocolate/Serves 2

225ml/7 1/2 fl oz milk
50g/2oz dark chocolate (70% cocoa solids)
2 tbsps caster sugar (optional)
1/2 tbsp cornflour
2 tbsps of milk

Directions

1. Break the dark chocolate into pieces. Put the chocolate, 200ml milk and sugar (if required) into a pan and moderately heat to melt the chocolate – do not boil. Whilst heating, mix the cornflour with the remaining milk to a paste-like consistency.

2. Once the chocolate has melted in the pan of milk, stir in the cornflour mix and heat for a further couple of minutes, or until the chocolate milk has thickened. Once ready, pour into cups and serve.

Wickedly White Chocolate Cake/Serves 10

150g/5 oz self raising flour, sifted
225g/8 oz caster sugar
125g/4 3/4 oz natural yoghurt
40g/1 1/2 oz cocoa powder, sifted
100g/4 oz butter (softened)
5 tbsps boiling water
2 large sized eggs
1 tsp baking powder

Decoration
275g/9 1/2 oz white chocolate
260ml/9 oz double cream
90g/3 1/2 oz dark chocolate

Directions – Cake

1. Preheat the oven to 180°C/350°F/Gas mark 4. Grease two 20cm sandwich tins and line their bases.

2. Place the cocoa powder into a large mixing bowl and add boiling water.

3. Mix until the mixture is smooth and leave to cool slightly for a couple of minutes.

4. Add into the mixture your eggs, sugar, flour, yoghurt, butter and baking powder, then beat thoroughly until you have a creamy texture.

5. Pour into the two cake tins, in equal amounts and smooth the surfaces of each so that they are level.

6. Place in the oven and cook for between 25 – 30 minutes, or until firm when touched.

Directions – Decoration

1. Break the white chocolate up into squares and place in a medium bowl. Heat the double cream to boiling point in a pan and then pour over the white chocolate.

2. Leave the cream to melt the chocolate for a few minutes and then stir the cream and chocolate together.

3. Leave to cool for 5-10 minutes, then whisk until thick and creamy. Once the cakes are cold, spread on half of the white chocolate mix and sandwich together.

4. Using the other half of the mix spread over the top and sides of the cake.

Chocolate Mousse Delight/Serves 8

400g/14 oz dark chocolate
210ml/4 fl oz double cream
6 eggs, separated
50g/2 oz caster sugar
2 tbsps brandy
2 tbsps icing sugar
4 amaretti biscuits, crushed

Directions

1. Firstly, melt the chocolate in a glass bowl either in the microwave, (on defrost setting) or over a saucepan of boiling water. Separate all 6 eggs and mix 4 of the yolks together. Discard the remaining 2 yolks. Keep the 6 whites for use later in the recipe.

2. Stir in 4-5 tbsps of the melted chocolate to the yolks and mix in well. After mixing, pour the chocolate and yolk mix into the remaining melted chocolate and mix thoroughly. Whip the cream lightly and add the brandy, (if required).

3. Carefully fold 1/3 of the whipped cream into the chocolate mix. Then add the chocolate mixture into the remaining cream. Whisk all six egg whites until 'rough' looking. Add in the caster sugar & gently fold into the chocolate mixture.

4. Carefully spoon the mousse into bowls and allow to chill for 1 hour. Finally, just prior to serving, sprinkle the mousse with icing sugar & the crushed amaretti biscuits.

Chocolate and Banana Smoothie/Serves 2

2 chopped bananas
2 scoops of chocolate icecream
2 tsps of instant coffee
1/4 pint of milk
8 ice cubes
chocolate sauce to decorate

Directions

1. Crush the ice and place in a blender with the chopped bananas, milk, instant coffee, and icecream. Blend until smooth.

2. Drizzle chocolate sauce along the inside of two tall glasses, add the smoothie and enjoy!

Tiramisu Treat/Serves 4

100g/4 oz dark chocolate
142ml 4 3/4 fl oz double cream
50ml/2 fl oz Tia Maria®, or preferred coffee liqueur
100g/4 oz sponge fingers
25g/1 oz caster sugar
25g/1 oz cocoa powder
1 tbsp of instant coffee
250ml/8 fl oz mascarpone cheese
3 chocolate flakes
1 tsp gelatine

Directions

1. To prepare, line the base and sides of a loose based cake tin. Dissolve the gelatine in a small amount of hot water. Add the sugar and coffee together and mix with 1 tbsp of boiling water. Add this to the gelatine, followed by 1 tbsp of your chosen liqueur.

2. Take the sponge fingers and dip them into the remaining liqueur. Line the cake tin with the sponge fingers and space the chocolate flakes around the outside edge.

3. Break the chocolate into a bowl and heat over a pan of simmering water. Leave to cool. Add the mascarpone cheese and coffee mixture together and whisk. Whisk in the double cream and cooled chocolate until it thickens. Carefully spoon the mixture into the cake tin and refrigerate overnight.

4. Before serving, gently remove from the tin onto a plate and sprinkle the top with the cocoa powder.

Marvellous Mississippi Mud Pie/Serves 8

25g/1 oz cocoa powder
225g/8 oz plain flour
25g/1 oz caster sugar
150g/5 1/2 oz butter
2 tbsps cold water

Filling mix
150g/5 1/2 oz dark chocolate
175g/6 oz butter
350g/12 1/2 oz dark muscovado sugar
300ml single cream
4 medium sized eggs, beaten
4 tbsp cocoa powder
1 tsp chocolate flavouring

Decoration
425ml/14 1/2 fl oz double cream, whipped
Bar of dark chocolate (approx. 100g)

Directions – Base

1. Preheat the oven to 190C/375F/Gas mark 5. Sieve the cocoa powder and flour into a mixing bowl. Mix in the butter and rub together until the mixture looks like breadcrumbs. Add the sugar and water, as needed, and mix in to make a soft dough. Refrigerate for 20 minutes.

2. Remove from the refrigerator and roll out the dough to fit into a 9 inch loose-bottomed flan tin. Line the tin with the pastry dough and line with baking paper and weigh down with baking beans. Place in the oven for 15 minutes.

3. Remove from the oven and take off the baking beans and baking paper. Return to the oven and bake for a further 10 minutes.

Directions – Filling

1. Take the oven temperature down to 160C/325F/Gas mark 3. Add the sugar and butter and beat in a bowl. Carefully beat in the eggs and cocoa powder.

2. Break the chocolate into a bowl and heat over a pan of simmering water until melted. Beat the melted chocolate into the mixture, adding the single cream and chocolate flavouring.

3. Pour the mixture into the pastry base and place in the oven at the reduced oven temperature for 15 minutes, or until the filling has set. Remove from the oven and leave to cool completely.

Directions – Decoration

1. Cover well with the whipped double cream and grate chocolate shavings over the top. Refrigerate for an hour before serving.

Chocolate Fondue and Fruit/Serves 4

125g/4 1/2 oz dark chocolate (broken into pieces)
120ml/4 fl oz double cream
Selection of sliced fruits (depending on taste)

Directions

1. Place the broken chocolate into a bowl, add the cream and place over a medium heat until melted. Be careful not to boil.

2. Pour the chocolate fondue mixture into a serving bowl and place on a large plate. Take the sliced fruit and arrange them decoratively around the edge, ready for dipping.

Chocolate & Coffee Liqueur Pots/Serves 8

300g/10 oz dark chocolate
500g/18 oz mascarpone cheese
284ml/9 1/2 fl oz whipped cream
12 tbsps coffee liqueur
10 tbsps icing sugar
Dark chocolate decorations, or grated chocolate

Directions

1. Break the chocolate into a bowl and heat over a pan of simmering water to melt the chocolate. Stir and remove from the heat once melted and smooth. Leave to cool.

2. Whisk the whipped cream until it creates soft peaks and stir in the coffee liqueur.

3. Add the mascarpone cheese and icing sugar together and beat well until smooth. Gently stir in the coffee/cream mixture and then pour over the cooled melted chocolate.

4. Mix with a fork, making swirling patterns – do not mix too well, keep the contrast of colours.

5. Spoon the mixture into 8 small serving pots and chill in the fridge. Before serving decorate with chocolate decorations or grated chocolate.

Rich Chocolate Chilli Truffles/Serves 8–10

700g/1 1/2 lb dark chocolate
400ml/14 fl oz double cream
30g/1 1/4 oz butter
50g/2 oz cocoa powder
Pinch of cinnamon and allspice
10 cloves
2 tbsps whiskey or rum
1 tsp dried chilli flakes
1 tbsp golden syrup

Directions

1. To prepare, grease a baking tin with oil and line with clingfilm.

2. Using a mortar and pestle grind the cinnamon, cloves, allspice and chilli.

3. Add to the double cream in pan and heat gently – do not boil. Add in the chocolate and stir, melt completely whilst still taking care not to boil. Stir in the whiskey or rum and the butter and golden syrup. Carefully pour the mixture into the tin and level off the top. Freeze for at least 1 hour.

4. Remove from the freezer and turn out onto a clean working surface. Remove the cling film and cut into 2cm cubes. Sift the cocoa powder into a bowl and toss the cubes, covering them with the powder. Serve or refrigerate until required.

Rum 'n' Raisin Chocolate Truffles/Makes 14–16

100g/4 oz dark chocolate
30g/1 oz raisins
2 tbsps rum
75ml/3fl oz double cream
20g/3/4 oz softened butter

Directions

1. Soak the raisins in the rum and leave to stand for 10 minutes. Break the chocolate into a bowl and heat over a pan of simmering water until melted.

3. Heat the double cream until at boiling point and then add to the melted chocolate. Beat in half of the softened butter, when mixed beat in the remaining half.

4. Mix in the rum and raisins and leave to cool. Dampen your hands and roll the mixture into small balls. Roll in cocoa powder and place on a serving dish. Refrigerate for approximately 30 minutes, or until set.

Ginger & Dark Chocolate Truffles/Makes 12

75g/3 oz dark chocolate
225g/8 oz ginger cake (broken into crumbs)
275g/10 oz grated white chocolate (refrigerated)
1 tbsp of cocoa powder
2 tbsps of orange marmalade
1 tbsp of rum

Directions

1. Lay out a sheet of greaseproof paper. Grate the white chocolate into a freezer safe container and freeze 15 minutes before starting to mix the truffle mixture.

2. Mix all of the other ingredients together in a bowl to a dough-like consistency. Remove the white chocolate from the freezer. Roll the doughy mixture into truffle-sized balls and roll in the white chocolate.

3. Alternatives could include rolling in nuts or perhaps coating the truffles in melted chocolate, leaving them to set on greaseproof paper before serving. You can also simply dust with cocoa powder.

Chocolate Marshmallows/Serves 2-4

100g/3 1/2 oz marshmallows
100g/3 1/2 oz dark chocolate
packet of cocktail sticks

1. Spike each marshmallow with a cocktail stick.

2. Break the chocolate into pieces and add to a bowl over a pan of simmering water. Heat until the chocolate is melted and then pour out into a serving bowl.

3. Dip the marshmallows into the chocolate sauce and arrange on a serving plate, ready to eat.

4. Before the chocolate dries you can add extra toppings such as grated coconut or chopped nuts.

5. You can also substitute the dark chocolate for milk or white chocolate, or even make a mixed plate of each variety.

125g/4 oz dark chocolate
100g/3 1/2 oz petit beurre biscuits
100g/3 1/2 oz sifted icing sugar
3 tbsps double cream
2 eggs, separated
50g/2 oz peeled red grapes
3 tbsps cooking kirsch
2 tbsps water
100g/3 1/2 oz unsalted butter

Directions

1. Oil a 13cm/5in sliding-based cake tin and line with lightly oiled greaseproof paper. Place the biscuits into a bowl, adding the cooking kirsch. Leave to soak.

2. Add the chocolate and water into a pan and melt over a medium heat whilst stirring. Do not boil. Once smooth, remove from the heat.

3. Cut the butter into small pieces and stir into the hot chocolate mix until dissolved.

5. Add in the egg yolks and beat until the mixture is smooth.

6. Stir in the sugar and mix well. Whip the egg whites until stiff and add to the mixture, beating them in thoroughly. Add in the kirsch soaked biscuits and grapes. Finally, add the cream and mix.

7. Turn the mixture out into the oiled cake tin and pat the surface level. Place in the refrigerator and leave for at least 2 hours, allowing the mixture to set.

8. Remove from the refrigerator and turn out onto a serving plate. Remove the greaseproof paper and decorate if desired. Serve by cutting into slices.

Luxury Chocolate Fudge Cake/Serves 8

65g/2 1/2 oz luxury Belgian chocolate
125g/4 1/2 oz plain flour
65g/2 1/2 oz brown sugar
65g/2 1/2 oz caster sugar
65g/2 1/2 oz butter
150ml/5fl oz milk
1 large egg, separated
1/2 tsp of bicarbonate of soda

Chocolate Fudge icing
65g/2 1/2 oz icing sugar
15g/1/2 oz butter
1 tbsp of milk
1/2 tbsp cocoa powder

Directions

1. Preheat the oven to 180°C/350°F/Gas mark 4. Line and grease a medium sized baking tin. Line the paper so that it comes up to 3cm above the edge on 2 opposite sides. Place 2 tbsps of milk, the brown sugar and chocolate together in a pan and stir over a medium heat until the sugar and chocolate have melted. Stir in the remaining milk. Mix the caster sugar and butter together until light in consistency and then beat in the egg yolk.

2. Take the bicarbonate of soda and flour, sift them together and stir into the butter/sugar mix. Mix the butter/sugar mixture with the chocolate/sugar mixture and beat together until smooth and creamy. Take the egg white and whisk it until peaks form. Gently fold in a tbsp of the egg white into the prepared mixture and then gradually fold in the remaining amount.

3. Place the mixture into the baking tin and bake for 50 minutes. Test by touching with your fingertips and check the cake springs back up.. Turn the cake out onto a wire cooling rack and leave to cool until tepid

Directions - Icing

1. Place a tbsp of milk and the butter into a small pan and heat until melted. Do not boil. Sift the cocoa powder and icing sugar together and add to the pan. Mix until smooth. Pour the mixture over the still-warm cake and spread over the top. Allow the icing to set before cutting into 8 even squares.

275g/9 1/2 oz sifted strong flour (for bread making)
30g/1oz butter
65g/2 1/2 oz dark chocolate (finely chopped)
Pinch of salt
3g or 1/2 sachet dried yeast
1/4 pint warm water
1/2 tsp honey

Directions

1. Take all of the ingredients, with the exception of the water and chocolate, and mix together in a large bowl. Once mixed, pour in the warm water and mix until a dough is formed.

2. Once mixed, pour in the warm water and mix until a dough is formed.

3. Turn out onto a lightly floured working surface and knead for approximately 10 minutes, or until it springs back. Push the chopped chocolate into the dough, spreading it evenly throughout.

4. Mould the dough into a loaf baking tin and brush with egg or milk. Cover with a damp tea towel and leave in a warm place until the dough has doubled in size. Whilst waiting for the dough to increase in volume, preheat the oven to 220C/425F/Gas mark 7.

7. Bake in the oven for 20-30 minutes, until golden in colour. Leave to cool for a short time and then turn out onto a wire cooling rack. To test whether cooked, tap the bottom of the loaf, if cooked it should sound hollow.

Dark Chocolate Amaretti Cake/Serves 10

180g/6 oz dark chocolate
425ml/15 fl oz double cream
350g/12 oz amaretti biscuits
4 tbsps brandy
3 tbsps cider
Cocoa powder (for dusting)

Directions

1. Break the chocolate into a bowl, add the cream and heat over a pan of simmering water until the chocolate is melted. Remove from the heat and whisk together with a hand-held mixer, until the mixture is creamy.

2, Mix the cider and brandy together and add to a small bowl. Take one of the biscuits and dip it into the liqueur and then into the chocolate cream.

3. Pop the biscuit at the base of a large pudding bowl and repeat the process, creating a layer of biscuits on the base. Spread a layer of the chocolate cream mixture over the layer of biscuits and repeat this until there are 4 layers, finishing with a layer of chocolate cream.

4. Place a plate on top of the layers, using a plate that fits inside the rim of the bowl. Weight the plate down with a few lbs and refrigerate. Leave overnight.

5. To serve, remove from the refrigerator and dip the bowl into a bowl of hot water for about 5 seconds.

6. Remove and turn the pudding out on to a serving plate. Return to the fridge for approximately 30 minutes. Dust with cocoa powder and serve.

Chocolate Chip Cookies

60g/2 1/4 oz dark chocolate, chopped finely
110g/4 1/4 oz soft unsalted butter
110g/4 1/4 oz plain flour
55g/2 oz caster sugar
30g/1 3/4 oz custard powder
1 tsp vanilla essence
Grated orange rind

Directions

1. Preheat the oven to 180C/350F/Gas Mark 4. Place the butter, vanilla essence and orange rind into a mixing bowl. Sieve the flour, caster sugar and custard powder into the same bowl and beat until thoroughly mixed.

2. Spoon out mixture one at a time and roll into small balls. Place the balls onto a baking tray and flatten. Bake in the oven for 25 minutes, or until cooked.

3. Remove from the oven and leave to cool on a wire cooling rack. Sprinkle with caster sugar, if desired.

Chocolate Mint Biscuits/Makes 30

300g/10 oz dark chocolate (broken into pieces)
100g/4 oz dark chocolate (to melt)
200g/7 oz porridge oats
200g/7 oz softened unsalted butter
150g/5 oz light soft brown sugar
130g/4 3/4 oz sifted self-raising flour
2 large eggs (beaten)
1 tsp baking powder
40g/1 1/2 oz fresh mint leaves (stalks removed)

Directions

1. Preheat the oven to 180°C/350°F/Gas mark 4. Place the sugar and butter into a food processor bowl and cream together. Add in the flour, egg, oats, baking powder and mint leaves, mixing them in, in short bursts. Once mixed in, add the 300g of chocolate and process again.

2. Flour your hands, take a tbsp of the mixture and shape into a ball. Flatten the mixture out to approximately 6cm in diameter and place on a piece of baking paper, (on a baking tray). Repeat the process until all the mixture is used.

3. Bake in the oven for 10 minutes. Remove from the oven and allow to cool for 5 minutes. Transfer the biscuits to a wire cooling rack and continue to cool.

4. Break the 100g of chocolate into a bowl and heat over a pan of simmering water until melted. Once the biscuits are cool, drizzle the melted chocolate decoratively over them and add a sprinkle of sieved icing sugar if desired.

Chocolate Caramel Biscuit/Serves 8

Chocolate Caramel Shortcake/Serves 8

Base
225g/8 oz self-raising flour
110g/4 oz caster sugar
170g/6 oz margarine

Filling
110g/4 oz butter
110g/4 oz sugar
400ml/14 fl oz condensed milk
2 tbsps golden syrup

Topping
170g/6oz dark chocolate

Directions

1. Preheat the oven to 180C/350F/Gas mark 4. Add the butter and sugar together and cream. Add in the flour and mix well.

2. Turn out into a cake tin and press down firmly. Bake for 20 minutes. Remove from the oven and leave to cool.

3. Add the butter, sugar, condensed milk and syrup into a pan and heat. Simmer for approximately 10 minutes.

4. Once thickened pour out and spread over the cooked base. Leave to cool.

5. Break the chocolate into a bowl and heat over a pan of simmering water until melted. Pour out over the caramel and spread evenly.

6. Leave to cool and then refrigerate for 1 hour to set. Cut into eight pieces.

Chocolate and Orange Tartlets/Serves 8

Pastry
350g/12 oz plain flour
170g/6 oz butter (cubed)
50g/2 oz caster sugar
2 egg yolks
1 tbsp of water

Filling
2 medium sized eggs
2 egg yolks
100g/4 oz caster sugar
200g/7 oz dark chocolate
50g/2 oz butter
2 tbsps of double cream
100ml/4fl oz orange liqueur

Directions – Pastry case

1. Add the flour, sugar, butter and egg yolk into a food processor and blend until the mixture looks like breadcrumbs. Add the water, preferably whilst the processor is going, and blend until the mixture turns into a ball of dough. Remove from the processor, wrap in cling film and leave for at least 30 minutes.

2. Break the dough into 8 similar-sized balls and roll it out onto a floured surface to about a 2-3mm thickness. Line 8 greased tartlet cases with the pastry mix, cover over and refrigerate for 20-30 minutes.

3. Whilst the pastry is in the refrigerator pre-heat the oven to 180C/350F/Gas mark 4. Once chilled, line each pastry case with greaseproof paper and weigh down with baking beans.

4. Bake for 10 minutes and then remove to take off the beans and greaseproof paper. Return to the oven for 10 minutes, then leave to cool

Directions – Filling

1. Whisk the egg yolk, egg and sugar together until the mixture is pale and has doubled in volume. Add the butter, cream, chocolate and liqueur to a bowl and heat over a pan of hot water – be careful not to boil the water as this will separate the mixture in the bowl. Fold the melted mixture into the eggs and mix thoroughly, folding as you go.

2. Pour the mixture into the pastry cases and bake in the oven for 15 minutes. Remove from the oven and leave to cool. Once cooled remove from their cases and serve.

White Chocolate Strawberry Skewers/Makes 8-10

600g/1 pint luxury white chocolate
4-5 punnets of strawberries

Directions

1. To prepare, line a baking tray with baking paper. Break the chocolate into a bowl and heat over a pan of simmering water until melted. Remove from the heat and stir until smooth.

2. Take each strawberry and dip them into the melted chocolate, allow the drips to fall back into the bowl. Push onto a skewer and add more, leaving enough room to hold the end of the skewer. Place the skewers onto the baking tray and set to one side in a cool place to allow the chocolate to set. Refrigerate to chill, if desired.

Chocolate & Banana Mousse/Serves 8

1 banana, (chopped)
200g/7 oz dark chocolate
1/2 tbsp of double cream
170g/6 oz mascarpone cheese
Squeeze of lemon juice
1 tbsp of shredded fresh mint leaves
Dash of rum

Directions

1. Add the cream and chocolate into a bowl and heat over a pan of simmering water until melted.

2. Add the mascarpone, mint leaves, lemon juice, banana and rum together in a bowl; beat thoroughly until well combined. Stir in the melted chocolate.

3. Pour the mixture equally into dessert bowls and refrigerate for 30 minutes. Remove from the refrigerator and serve.

Chocolate Dream/Serves 4-6

300ml/1/2 pint single cream
300ml/1/2 pint double cream
100g/4 oz white breadcrumbs
115g/4 1/2 oz Demerara sugar
2 tbsps coffee
8 tbsps hot chocolate

Directions

1. Whip both creams together until they are light and fluffy.

2. Add the sugar, coffee, breadcrumbs, and hot chocolate in a bowl and mix well. Place a layer of the breadcrumb mix in the bottom of a serving bowl, followed by a layer of the cream.

3. Repeat the process to the top of the bowl, ending with a cream layer. Refrigerate overnight to set and decorate with crumbled chocolate flake before serving.

Chocolate Apples on Sticks/Serves 6

6 medium sweet-tart apples, such as Braeburn, Fuji, or Gala
6 round lolly sticks
200g/7 oz dark chocolate
200g/7 oz white chocolate
Chopped nuts, coconut, caramel for additional topping (optional)

Directions

1. Prepare the apples, by washing and piercing with the lolly sticks. You can twist of the stalks if you wish. Then place the apples in the fridge while preparing the chocolate covering as they will coat better if they're cold.

2. In two separate pans, slowly melt the chocolate over hot water or in a microwave set on high for 2 minutes, stirring halfway through the heating time to smooth it out. Do not allow the chocolate to boil.

3. Remove from the heat and stir until completely melted and warm, not hot. Holding the apples by the sticks, dunk each apple into the chocolate, allowing the excess to drip back into the pan. Roll the apples around in the chocolate, turning with the stick, so it's coated all the way up to the top. Use a spoon to baste any hard to get spots.

4. Put the desired coating in a separate bowl and roll the dipped apple around so it is completely covered. Set the chocolate dipped apples on a baking tray or plate with wax paper and then refrigerate until the chocolate is set. If you want to decorate your apples with chocolate drizzles wait until the chocolate is set then reheat the remaining chocolate sauce in the pan and then drizzle over, and refrigerate again before serving.

Chocolate Fudge Liqueur Sauce

200g/7oz dark chocolate
400g/14 oz condensed milk
1 tbsp golden syrup
2 tbsps Grand Marnier®
2 tbsps cold water

Directions

1. Break the chocolate into a pan and add the golden syrup, condensed milk, Grand Marnier and water.

2. Heat and gently stir occasionally until the ingredients are melted and well mixed.

3. Pour into a jug to serve warm, or store in a container and refrigerate. To serve once refrigerated, warm over a gentle heat. Use within 2 weeks of making. This sauce is delicious when served as a warm dipping sauce with fruit.

Mini Chocolate Souffles/Makes 12

Sauce
200g/7 oz sugar
100g/4 oz cocoa powder
200ml/7 fl oz crème fraiche
12 slices candied orange

Soufflé
200g/7 oz dark chocolate
200g/7 oz icing sugar
120g/4 1/2 oz butter
65g/2 1/2 oz cocoa powder
8 eggs, separated

Directions – Sauce

1. Lightly grease 12 ramekins. Place the sugar and broken chocolate in a pan and heat gently. Gradually add in the crème fraiche, stirring continuously. Cook until the volume is reduced by half.

Directions – Souffles

1. Preheat the oven to 190C/375F/Gas mark 5. Break the chocolate into a bowl and heat over a pan of simmering water until melted. Add in the butter and egg yolks and mix.

2. Whisk the egg whites until stiff, then add in the sugar and carry on whisking. Add this to the chocolate mixture, little by little. Lightly grease 12 ramekins. Spoon out the mixture into the ramekins to three-quarters full. Bake in the oven for 8-10 minutes. Do not open the door whilst cooking!

4. Remove from the oven and decorate the top with the strips of the candied orange and dust with icing sugar and serve with chocolate sauce.

Saucy Chocolate Pudding/Serves 4

Pudding
50g/2 oz luxury dark chocolate
(already melted and cooled)
120g/4 1/2 oz caster sugar
120g/4 1/2 oz self-raising flour
120g/4 1/2 oz unsalted butter
2 large eggs
2 tbsps of vanilla essence
Icing sugar (to decorate)

Sauce mix
75g/3 oz luxury plain chocolate
75g/3 oz dark brown sugar
200ml/7fl oz water
1 tsp of vanilla essence
1 tbsp of sifted cocoa powder

Directions

1. Firstly, preheat the oven to 180°C/350°F/Gas mark 4. Grease a shallow 900ml ovenproof dish, ready for the pudding mixture. Place all of the pudding ingredients into a large bowl and beat or whisk, until the mixture is of a creamy consistency. Carefully spoon the mixture into the ovenproof dish and level the top, leaving room for the sauce to be poured on.

2. Place all of the sauce ingredients into a bowl and simmer over water to melt. Stir the mixture and remove from heat when fully blended. Pour the sauce onto the pudding mixture.

3 Place in the oven and bake for 40-50 minutes. To test, en   the sponge has risen and the sauce has sunk to the bottom of the pudding. Finish by dusting with icing sugar before serving.

Chocolate, Date and Walnut Pudding/Serves 4-6

25g/1 oz chopped dates
25g/1 oz chopped walnuts
3 tbsps plain wholemeal flour
2 eggs, separated
2 tbsps golden caster sugar
1 tsp vanilla essence
1 tbsp cocoa powder
30ml/1 fl oz milk

Directions

1. To prepare, grease a 1.2 litre pudding basin and place a small circle of non-stick baking paper in the base. Preheat the oven to 180C/350F/Gas mark 4. Add the walnuts and dates to the bottom of the pudding basin.

2. Place the egg yolks, sugar and vanilla in a bowl and heat over a pan of hot water. Whisk until the mixture is thick and pale. Remove from the pan of hot water and sift the cocoa powder and flour into the bowl and fold in gently with a metal spoon. Whisk the egg whites until they create soft peaks and fold them into the mixture.

3. Spoon the mixture into the basin and bake in the oven for 40-45 minutes, or until well risen and firm to the touch. Leave to cool a little for 10 minutes. Run a knife carefully around the edge of the basin and turn the pudding out onto a serving plate. Serve warm with Greek yoghurt, custard, cream or icecream, if desired.

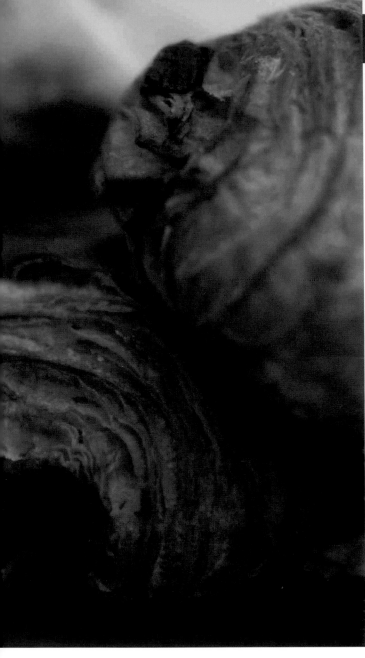

Pain au Chocolat/Serves 8

115g/4 oz dark chocolate, finely chopped
250g/9 oz white bread flour
100g/3 1/2oz butter
25g/1 oz caster sugar
175ml/6fl oz milk
2 tsps dried yeast
1 tsp salt
1 tbsp vegetable oil
1 egg yolk
1 1/2 tbsps of milk

Directions

1. To prepare, line a baking tray with a sheet of greased baking paper. Sprinkle flour onto a clean working surface. Sift the flour and salt into a bowl, stir in the yeast and mix. Create a well in the middle of the mixture.

2. Heat the milk in a pan until just warm in temperature, then add in the oil and sugar. Stir well until the ingredients have completely dissolved. Add to the flour/salt/yeast and mix to a doughy consistency.

3. Take the mixture out of the bowl and knead until smooth. Oil a bowl and place the dough inside. Cover with a tea towel and leave in a warm place for 2-3 hours, during which time the dough will double in volume.

4. Re-flour the working surface and remove the dough from the covered bowl. Knead the dough and roll into a rectangular shape, 3 times as long as it is wide.

5. Cut the butter into thirds and place one cut of butter over two-thirds of the rolled out dough, making sure to leave a 1cm border around the edges. Carefully fold the lower-third of the dough up and the lower-third down and seal the edges down. Half turn the dough and roll it into a rectangular shape. Repeat this process twice more and then fold the dough in half. Place the dough in an oiled polythene bag and refrigerate for 1 hour. Preheat the oven to 220C/425F/Gas mark 7.

6. Remove the dough from the refrigerator and take out of the polythene bag. Cut the dough in half and roll out into 2 rectangular shapes of 30cm x 15cm. Cut each of the rectangles into 4 rectangles of approximately 15cm x 8cm.

7. Take the chopped dark chocolate and sprinkle over one short end of each rectangle and roll up into a roll. Place the rolls onto the greased baking sheet, cover with a tea towel and leave in warm place for 2-3 hours.

8. Mix the egg yolk and milk together and glaze each of the rolls. Bake in the oven for 18-20 minutes. Remove from the oven and serve either warm or cold.

Fruity Chocolate Refrigerator Cake/Serves 8

225g/8 oz ginger nut biscuits, broken
175g/6 oz dark chocolate
25g/1 oz sultanas
25g/1 oz glace cherries, chopped
25g/1 oz dried cherries
25g/1 oz mixed peel
25g/1 oz flaked almonds
140g/5 oz unsalted butter
4 tbsps double cream

Directions

1. To prepare, line a cake tin with foil and brush the foil lightly with oil. Mix the biscuits, various fruits, peel and almonds in a bowl.

2. Add the butter, cream and chocolate to a pan and place over a low heat, stir until the chocolate is melted and the mixture is smooth.

3. Pour the melted chocolate mix over the biscuit/fruit mix and stir together well. Spoon the mixture into the cake tin and press down firmly and evenly.

4. Cover the cake mix with foil and refrigerate for 2 1/2 hours. Remove from the refrigerator and turn out onto a plate, peeling off the foil. To serve, cut into slices and serve with fresh fruit pieces and icecream.

Double-Chocolate Crispy Squares/Makes approximately 30

White chocolate layer
300g/10 oz white chocolate
100g/4 oz Rice Crispies cereal
8 tbsps butter
2 tbsps golden syrup

Dark chocolate layer
250g/9 oz dark chocolate
150g/5 oz Rice Crispies cereal
8 tbsps butter
4 tbsps golden syrup

Directions

1. To prepare, grease 2 x 8-10 inch square cake tin and line with baking paper. Break the white chocolate into a bowl and add the golden syrup and butter. Heat over a pan of simmering water and stir until melted. Remove from the heat and stir in the Rice Crispies, covering them well.

2. Turn out into the 2 cake tins and press down gently. Break the dark chocolate into a bowl and add the golden syrup and butter. Heat over a pan of simmering water and stir until melted. Remove from the heat and stir in the Rice Crispies, covering them well.

3. Turn out over the white chocolate layer in both tins and press down gently to even the surface a little. Once cooled, refrigerate for 2 hours. When chilled and hard, turn out of the tin and cut into evenly shaped squares. Place on a serving plate to serve.

Chocolate Fudge Cupcakes/Makes 24

Cake
200g/7 oz golden caster sugar
130g/5 oz dark chocolate (broken)
350ml/12 fl oz milk
300g/10 oz self-raising flour
130g/5 oz softened, butter
4 tbsps chocolate chips
1 beaten egg
2 tsp vanilla extract

Fudge icing
250g/8 oz dark chocolate
70g/2 1/2 oz softened butter
2 tbsps golden syrup

Directions

1. Line 2 mini-cake tins with 24 paper cases, (12 in each). Preheat the oven to 180°C/350F/Gas mark 4. Place 1/3 of the sugar and the chocolate in a bowl. Heat the milk and when simmering pour over the chocolate and sugar and stir.

2. Add the butter, remaining sugar and vanilla together and beat well until the mixture is pale and fluffy. Stir in the beaten egg and beat for a couple of minutes. Mix in the chocolate mixture, chocolate chips and flour. Spoon the well mixed mixture into the paper cases and place in the oven for 20 minutes. Remove and leave to cool.

3. For the icing, break the chocolate into a bowl and heat over a bowl of simmering water to melt. Once melted remove from the heat and stir in the golden syrup and butter. Leave to cool until the mixture has just set and then ice the tops of each of the cakes.

Double Chocolate-Chip Muffins

100g/4 oz cooking chocolate
300g 10 oz self raising flour (sifted)
1 tsp baking powder
100g/4 oz dark muscovado sugar
250ml/8 fl oz milk
50g/2 oz melted butter
2 eggs, beaten
50g/2 oz dark chocolate chips
50g/2 oz white chocolate chips

Directions

1. Preheat the oven to 200C/400F/Gas Mark 6. Break the chocolate into a bowl and heat over a pan of simmering water until melted.

2. Sift the flour and baking powder into a bowl. In a separate bowl add the muscovado sugar, melted chocolate, butter, milk and eggs and mix well. Carefully fold in the flour, taking care not to over-mix it. Stir in the dark and white chocolate chips.

3. Spoon the mixture into paper muffin cases and bake for 25 minutes, or until the muffins are risen and firm to the touch. Remove from the oven and leave to cool for 5 minutes. Transfer the muffins to a wire tray to continue cooling.

Chocolate Christmas Log/Serves 8

Cake
75g/3 oz milk chocolate
100g/4 oz mixed dried fruit
1 chocolate Swiss roll
50g/2 oz sifted icing sugar
25g/1 oz softened unsalted water
50g/2 oz crushed digestive biscuits
2 tbsp strawberry jam
1 tbsp of orange juice

Decoration
Icing sugar (for decoration)
Cocoa powder
Green and red food colouring
Fondant icing

Directions

1. Add the crushed biscuits, jam, dried fruit, and orange juice to a large bowl. Crumble in the Swiss roll and mix together thoroughly with your hands. Turn out the mixture onto a clean working surface and flatten and shape into a roll, approximately the same size as the Swiss roll. Wrap with cling film and refrigerate.

2. Shred 15-20g of the chocolate, (using either the edge of a cheese grater or potato peeler). Break the rest of the chocolate into pieces and place in a bowl, over simmering water to melt.

3. Beat the butter in a bowl and then add in and beat the melted chocolate, (ideally this will still be slightly warm). This will be your outer chocolate icing.

4. Remove the roll from the refrigerator and take out of the cling film. Spread the chocolate coating onto the log with a spreading knife. Using a fork scrape the icing to make it resemble tree bark. Sprinkle some icing sugar over the log for a snow effect.

5. For further decoration, place the log on a serving plate and sprinkle over the top the shredded chocolate. Colour some of the fondant icing red and some green, shape the green icing into leaf shapes and roll the red icing into berry-sized balls; decorate the log as holly sprigs. Sprinkle over a little more icing sugar if desired.

Easter Chocolate Crispy Cornflake Cups/Makes 12

3 1/2 tbsps butter
4 tbsps golden syrup
4 oz milk chocolate, chopped
100 gms cornflakes cereal
24-26 Cadburys mini-eggs®

Directions

1. In a saucepan over a low heat, combine the butter, golden syrup and chocolate. Cook and stir until butter and chocolate have melted and everything is well blended.

2. Mix in the cornflakes cereal. Drop by heaping spoonfuls onto waxed paper or a buttered baking sheet. Add a couple of mini eggs to the top and place in the refrigerator until set, about 15 minutes.

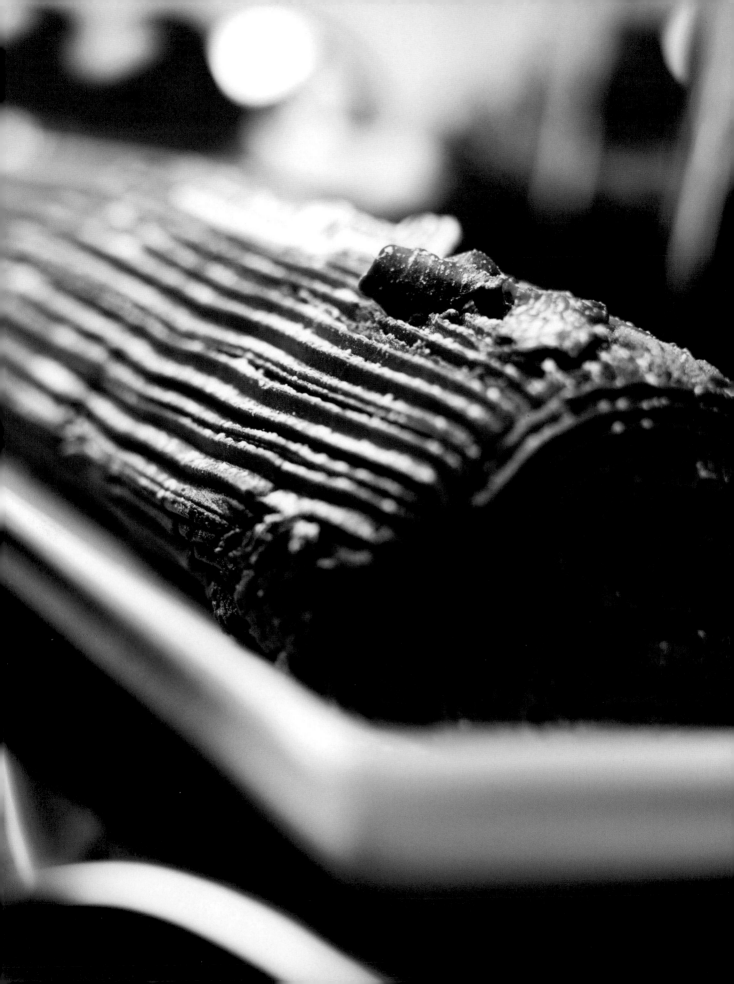

The recipes contained in this book are passed on in good faith but the publisher cannot be held responsible for any adverse results. Please be aware that certain recipes may contain nuts. The recipes use both metric and imperial measurements, and the reader should not mix metric and imperial measurements. Spoon measurements are level, teaspoons are assumed to be 5ml, tablespoons 15ml. For other measurements, see chart below. Times given are for guidance only, as preparation techniques may vary and can lead to different cooking times.

Spoons to millilitres

1/2 teaspoon	2.5 ml	1 Tablespoon	15 ml
1 teaspoon	5 ml	2 Tablespoons	30 ml
1-1 1/2 teaspoons	7.5 ml	3 Tablespoons	45 ml
2 teaspoons	10 ml	4 Tablespoons	60 ml

Grams to ounces

10g	0.25oz	225g	8oz
15g	0.38oz	250g	9oz
25g	1oz	275g	10oz
50g	2oz	300g	11oz
75g	3oz	350g	12oz
110g	4oz	375g	13oz
150g	5oz	400g	14oz
175g	6oz	425g	15oz
200g	7oz	350g	16oz

Metric to cups

Description		1 cup
Flour etc	115g	1 cup
Clear honey etc	350g	1 cup
Liquids etc	225ml	1 cup

Liquid measures

5fl oz	1/4 pint	150 ml
7.5fl oz		215 ml
10fl oz	1/2 pint	275 ml
15fl oz		425 ml
20fl oz	1 pint	570 ml
35fl oz		1 litre

This edition first published in 2009 by ImPulse Paperbacks, an imprint of Iron Press Ltd. © Iron Press Ltd 2009 Printed in China